Brackman

Mr. Robert Brackman's Studio Noank, Connecticut

BRACKMAN

HIS ART AND TEACHING

Kenneth Bates

MADISON ART GALLERY PUBLISHING COMPANY
in cooperation with
MR. ROBERT BRACKMAN

Library of Congress Cataloging in Publication Data

Bates, Kenneth, 1895-
  Brackman: his art and teaching.

  "The first one hundred copies of this edition are
numbered and signed by Robert Brackman."
  1. Brackman, Robert, 1898-   I. Title.
ND237.B77B3 1973   759.13   73-19805

Design by Heather Meredith-Owens

Production by Karen Gillis

Manufactured in the United States by Book Press, Brattleboro, Vermont

IN COOPERATION WITH

MR. ROBERT BRACKMAN

KENNETH BATES

MADISON ART GALLERY PUBLISHING COMPANY/ CONNECTICUT

193/73

To the memory of

ROBERT MACBETH

whose friendship and encouragement gave heart

to a generation of young artists.

ACKNOWLEDGMENTS

The publishers would like to offer their appreciation and gratitude to all the owners of Mr. Robert Brackman's oil paintings and pastel drawings which have been reproduced in this book without specific credit. They would also like to acknowledge Miss Heather Meredith-Owens' work in researching, authenticating and obtaining black and white and color reproductions of all of Mr. Brackman's works with which this book is adorned.

CONTENTS

PART ONE

Brackman, the Artist

I   The Times and the Artist   11

II   The Painter   16

III   The Still Lifes   23

IV   The Figure Paintings   28

V   The Portraits   35

PART TWO

Brackman, the Teacher

I   Brackman and the Student   44

II   The Approach   49

III   The Conception   57

IV   The Construction   65

V   The Underpainting   70

VI   The Color   74

Biography   82

Plates   87

PART ONE

Brackman, the Artist

In Abundance Oil 28″ x 36″ Courtesy of the Collection of
Mrs. Jascha Giller

I

The Times and the Artist

OUR CENTURY AND BRACKMAN HAVE GROWN UP AND MATURED TOGETHER. This is an appropriate time to take a brief glance back across those years which have seemed to us so exciting, not only because they are the ones we have personally experienced, but because they have been unusually vital ones in art history. Also, if we are to understand Brackman's present position in American art, we must see him in relation to the events of these years. Both as artist and teacher he has throughout maintained that whatever else painting may be it is first of all a craft with a great tradition, a skill to be acquired by which the artist's imagination is given means of expression. When most of the art world was being stampeded into extremes of experiment, he, almost alone, continued to maintain that tradition must first be learned, if for nothing more than to find how to break it intelligently. Admittedly, any periods in which great changes occur in man's thought or his environment are bound to produce similar upheavals in his art, if it is to serve as his cultural record; but in order to prove ourselves modern men it is hardly desirable to throw away everything learned in the past.

In every generation the arts strive to reflect the thought of the day. In painting, that usually results in the rise of a new school which stresses qualities neglected or frowned upon by its immediate predecessor; a battle ensues, and when all the tumult finally dies, it is found merely that two sides of the same truth have been expressed (complete truth being impossibly beyond any one system of thought) and both sides are eventually enshrined in the museums representing their period.

In our time, the differences between the various groups, not only in painting and sculpture but also in literature and architecture, were heightened because the entire Hellenic-Western tradition was under attack. Briefly, the new thesis was: we have uprooted many long established ideas about our universe and man's place in the scheme of things; time has become an added dimension of space; our idea of life itself has changed from a vitalistic to an energy concept. Our complex industrial, mechanized world is too far removed from the simple existence of classical days, with their humanized conception of nature, for the old cultural symbols to have any possible meaning. Modern man cannot see nymphs and dryads in his woods, and Jupiter tossing thunderbolts is no symbol of power for an atom-smashing age. We must find new, pure, free forms to serve our needs as the Greek forms expressed theirs. The whole representational, realistic art must make way for new expressions.

So the war was on, and after the first half century it looks much as if former patterns would hold true and the best of all the schools would, as usual, be lined up together in galleries, complementing and competing with each other. But this time the war has been so bitter that it is probable the ghosts of the artists will haunt the empty halls at night and carry on the battles.

Throughout all these years Brackman has been associated with no group movement, and, although his defense of the great tradition of European painting naturally places him somewhere on the conservative side of things, he has most certainly been aware of and influenced by the experimental art of the time, but not as a follower of a certain school. Phases of abstract art greatly stimulated his interest in a structural basis of a picture. A study of the old masters showed him that this was not new; it was to be found in all periods. Oddly enough, this affirmation of basic structure now separated his work from the bulk of the so-called academic work of the period, which certainly did not fit Webster's definition of academic, "rigid and formal, but full of knowledge," since it was painfully casual in following accidental surface appearances with what might be

called timid gusto. The Brackman work, with its classical sense of arrangement, was far away from this superficial spirit. He, however, deliberately went the way he had chosen and, as his work gained internal authority, it attracted increasingly serious attention, although at no time was he what might be called the painter of the year.

In the art world as in book publishing, song writing or in the theatre, it is common procedure to focus on a few spectacular hits, flood them with high-powered publicity for a period, and then go on to a new sensation. Certain trends are made into movements and people outside the classification are not in the current style. Since Brackman fitted in with neither the School of Paris nor the Regionalists, he avoided the most publicized art battle of the day. The School of Paris, in their efforts to create a new art, had done a great deal of experimental work which generated violent opposition. The appearance of several strong painters in the American realistic tradition was greeted as our answer, and, although they too were soundly based on European art, they were lined up as our present day "embattled farmers" to repel the European invasion. Fine paintings were made in both camps, so no harm was done and the Midwest had cause to rejoice in its new prestige.

Through these years art was put to the service of an odd assortment of

causes. During the depression the social revolt school swept through the country until every landscape had its brick walls and every figure study its human tragedy. When the political propaganda became too obvious the public lost interest.

The Surrealists, a Freudian offshoot of the internationalist group, attempted to bring art into the orbit of abnormal psychology, and for a time held the spotlight. Art has frequently produced a Hieronymous Bosch or a Lorenzo Lotto with highly original and unrealistic vision, but such work is too personal to pass on to hundreds of followers, and this cause died a-borning.

During all this Brackman has painted in his own way and, what is more, thought in his own way—a quality hard for some to understand. If told that the time to paint in the great tradition has passed, he says, in effect, that it takes more than the opinion of a few to make obsolete eight hundred years of great painting, and that the permanent value of current work will not be proven for another half century.

While some may use their art to advance political or social or psychological or other special ideas, he proposes to paint simple things needing no interpreter. If others choose to make mankind an object of loathing or pity, he unashamedly accepts a humanistic attitude, and by his work shows he considers humanity the most beautiful and exciting phenomenon in the world—with traces of nobility cropping out here and there. His young women have lyric beauty of form, and a kind of glory comes across the face of age. If present-day artists cannot look life in the face and find it good, so much the worse for them.

After trying to find an appropriate pigeon-hole for Brackman, the critics finally gave it up and said he had a timeless quality, which comes near the truth. Not that he claims to belong to the ages, but simply that for thirty years he has tried to get rid of everything casual and to build an art of qualities too permanent ever to be out of style. He has eschewed stylishness, and in the course of time style has been given him.

II
The Painter

TAKING CÉZANNE'S STATEMENT OF PURPOSE, "TO MAKE OF IMPRESSIONISM
an art as solid and durable as that of the museums," you have but to para-
phrase it slightly to get the purpose of Brackman's work, which is to make
of Impressionism, and the more recent research into the nature of form
and color, a contemporary art as solid and complete as that of the old
masters. He feels, again like Cézanne, that one should not substitute one's
self for the past, but merely add a new link. His attitude toward tradition
has to be understood if there is to be any appreciation of his work. Brackman does not feel stifled or hemmed in to be shut up in the same world
with eight hundred years full of painting—he loves it. In fact, there is
nothing to stimulate and thrill him like a really great picture painted by
some friend and fellow workman, even though he missed seeing that
particular friend by a few hundred years. The quality of his thought, his
solution of his painter's problems tell the present-day artist what manner
of man he was.

Brackman is more aware of this great stream of creative workers, they
are more real to him than the people he meets on the street, because their
expression reveals them more fully. He is simply but proudly struggling

Life and Still Life

OIL
50½″ x 40″
DELAWARE ART MUSEUM, DELAWARE

Girl from a Village

OIL
24″ x 30″
SPRINGVILLE MUSEUM OF ART, SPRINGVILLE, UTAH

Junior   OIL
                                                          84" x 160"
GRAND CENTRAL ART GALLERIES, NEW YORK, N.Y.

Portrait of My Friend

to create something worthy to hang alongside the greatest of them and represent his own day to some future Brackman just as Giotto, Titian, Rembrandt, Poussin and others reveal their several periods to him. They don't tie his hands or give him a sense of futility, or do any of the dire things they are supposed to; they are, instead, still living proofs that great things can be done, and they have been known to give a fellow some very shrewd advice on how it can be done. The only chains he sees that hold a man back are ignorance of what is fine and the lack of an adequate means of expression.

Here, it might be well to pause and see if we can find what Brackman considers that an artist needs to know, and, if possible, also find what he thinks makes a good painting. The obvious answer to that is, of course, to skip the text and turn to the plates which will tell, the only way an artist can, exactly what he thinks about it all. Unfortunately, not everyone can sight read a picture, and words, no matter how unsatisfactory they may be, are necessary to introduce us to the language of paint.

The artist is a craftsman, and paint is what he has to work with—brushes, paint and a rectangular flat plane—so what he builds on that canvas must be constructed out of paint. Any good craftsman soon learns to love the things he works with. He learns their nature, what beauties they have, what they can best be made to express; thinking and feeling in terms of his medium. A cabinet maker learns the nature of wood, and his work is great to the degree that his designs bring out the utmost of its peculiar power and beauty. This we all know to be true of workers in wood, stone, metal and other materials, but with the painter this truth is frequently forgotten, even by the artist himself.

He has other problems which complicate things, and the greatest of these is subject matter, which often makes such demands on him that he cannot show equal respect to it and his medium. Brackman's only dictum on subject is that whatever is chosen must be capable of being expressed better in paint than in any other way.

More will be learned about Brackman's ideas on art through a trip to the studio than by trying to extract a statement from him. What he has to say about painting he says with his paint brush. When he is planning a new picture, the visual images forming in his mind are in no sense arguments in support of some art theory he has concocted. Brackman's pictures are born as an image, develop, and are put onto canvas as an image and are seen and responded to as an image. They finish as they start, visual excitements to entice the eye.

When a lover's face is aglow, his words do not matter; everyone knows

what he means unless he really grows coherent. If Bob hears people talking art he watches to see if their faces light up with a spark of creative enthusiasm; if not, he pays no heed to their words. His scorn for rationalizing over art is something awesome and frightening to behold. He considers it a parlor game people resort to when their imaginations are too feeble to create pictures.

When met on the street and asked what he is doing, if his face lights up and his eyes sparkle and he explodes with something to the effect that "It's beautiful—you should see it!" you know it is time to leave him alone a few days and then go down and see the new picture. When his enthusiasm hits a new high, the picture will usually turn out to have done the same. This wholehearted delight in work on a new picture is the best assurance that the creative spark is being maintained, and that a work of art is really in formation.

When, after leaving him working on a still life at noon, he answered the phone at 3:30 with "You should see me! I'm working on a self portrait!" it was obviously the moment to catch the lay in of a new study. On the easel was a canvas which he insisted was only a 25″ x 30″, though it scaled up like a 30″ x 36″. It was completely designed, loosely painted, with a lot of white canvas showing in the lights, but in such condition that an hour's work defining the drawing would have put it in shape to be shown as a portrait sketch. It was a complete statement, with tremendous vitality in arrangement, but personal experience sitting for a portrait of the same size indicated that there would be at least fifteen more prolonged sittings. What happens needs to be explained.

No sketches had preceded this first lay in, but the whole theme had crystallized visually in his mind. It was now stated in color values as they appear in light, thinly brushed in to permit continued work. The drawing was indicated by color areas, but nowhere particularized.

Now comes the prolonged drive for the most vital possible statement, which he achieves by one thing: relationship. After the structure is redefined, the color tempo in the head is stepped up, then the figure. The now lifeless background is charged with vibrating tones until the figure in its turn appears unrealized. The next session, the form is again driven into a still more powerful range of opaque lights and transparent darks. This process continues at increased tempo until something seems bound to crack. Toward the end one feels as if Ravel's Bolero were being played in the room. At last the moment comes when the whole composition comes together as a unit and the work is done. Brackman lays down his brushes and says, "That is as far as this one will go; the next one we will push further."

The result of this method is that not only is the impression vivid but as time goes on the brilliant color, which throughout is under the darks, will retain all the present power. All relationships are as powerfully expressed as he can state them: lights to darks, surface texture against opposing texture. The energy with which he maintains this sustained drive is like a physical struggle. He demonstrates repeatedly that there is nothing that can be done to the form itself that will make it as real as what is done to the space around it. In figure studies by the thousands the area between the form and the frame is no man's land, and the form never comes out of it alive. Brackman's space has light in it but is not light; it has dark in it but is not dark, because light and dark are the opposing qualities of form.

This same method of work is used in whatever Brackman paints. To him there is no such thing as figure or still life painting, except for identification purposes. All painting is one and the same thing. He draws studies out of the racks to show what he means. The still lifes in various stages of completion, figures, interiors are all done the same way. Each, one notices, at every stage has the stamp of a genuine creation, even the ones that draw a menacing frown from him which bodes ill for them. There is always an abstract design on which the picture is built—despite the seem-

ingly realistic approach, which has made it hard to pin an appropriate label on him. But why succumb to the habit of classifying everything with the feeling that once we have given it a name we understand it?

Labels, however, are not always unappreciated. What would a new art movement ever do without a banner? Given a few good leaders and a rallying cry, the followers will gather in flocks. A cause is born, a grateful pack of writers is off in full cry over the warm scent, dealers are flooded with publicity and people. Cocktail parties can talk art without having to study it. The aesthetes move in and take over. A cause is something you can do something about, something to get radiant or apoplectic about, as the case may be. Imagine trying to get worked up about one artist alone trying to make the next picture just a little bit better than the last. Wherefore few choose to work alone; it is friendlier in a group. But causes soon lose their novelty; the idea now accepted or discarded can no longer be fought over and the label, once so bright and gay, is now dull and useless; but alas, it still sticks and cannot be lost. The one song sure to bore the public is last month's juke box favorite.

Just how a youngster in Brackman's place avoided these opportunities to wander off down some lane leading nowhere, it is hard to say. Arriving from Russia at twelve, there was a new language and a whole new way of living to be learned, also a living to be earned. All around him the most radical political, social and artistic ideas were being tossed into the air. Perhaps the very number of ready-made solutions put him on his guard. Certainly there is no trace at any time of an attempt to find a substitute for hard work along accepted lines. In fact, the pictures at first were not too different from those of a number of serious, talented youngsters who had learned in the schools to construct figure studies somewhat in the manner of the Impressionists, and were feeling their way cautiously toward a more personal expression.

To place an early Brackman beside a current example is to see some quite sharp contrasts. About all it says about Brackman is that he is keenly alive to the most vital art of the past generation and is determined to learn from it everything he can. It shows struggle, self-discipline of the severest sort, and his grim determination to batter a way through to a grasp of beauty, in pitched battle if necessary. The studied casualness and incidental gestures of the early figures, usually involved in the matter of getting dressed or undressed, are flattering tributes of a young artist to the great Impressionist masters, particularly Degas. The recent Brackman beside it could hardly be more different in spirit; it is as serene as a Chinese Buddha. Every statement is that of a mature painter and everything there is now completely his own, with authority evident in every part.

In the early work, objects frequently exist on their own. They are straight out of nature, of which the picture is but a fragment, arbitrarily stopped at the frame. Parts of figures, mirrors, tables or windows remain just that to the end. Looking at the recent work, we see what he means when he states and restates to his class that the artist's imagination is what changes an experience of nature into an experience of color based on nature, but with an existence and reality of its own. It sees those things his heart tells him are the truth, visualizes them in forms familiar to us all, and by his skill of hand and eye translates them into a new form which, if nobly conceived, may perchance live on past our day as our ambassadors to the future. To this end, at least, the artist has a right to struggle.

Still Life at Mystic   Oil   30″ x 36″   Private Collection

III

The Still Lifes

THE YOUNG ART STUDENT BELIEVES THAT HIS ABILITY TO CREATE GREAT
art is a matter of feeling and thinking which can be developed quite apart
from his actual painting; the world is full of exciting things and his head
is a jumble of thrilling ideas which he wants to express. He, of all people,
is least conditioned to enjoy the pleasures of still life painting. He invests
subject matter with exactly the glamor it has in life. To paint a beautiful
girl is to enjoy that beauty; to paint a bunch of carrots is to spend an afternoon looking at a bunch of carrots. When to that indignity is added the
undoubted difficulty of making oil paint do any of the things he is expected to make it do, his resentment at still life as an art form is easy to
understand. This is all most unfortunate because his teachers are quite
right in insisting that there is no better place to learn to paint. The student,
however, considers this to be merely the development of technique, something he would gladly trade for inspiring aesthetic ideas.

Brackman has a quite different idea about all this. He feels that creative imagination for the painter consists not in getting an idea for a picture and then spending weeks trying to figure out how to torture his paint
into expressing it, but in having in his mind such a storehouse of knowledge

of what can be made through paint, and how it can be made, that this craftsmanship is not only the means by which his ideas are expressed, but is also, what is vastly more exciting and important, the means by which the visual conception originates in his mind. There is no need to find a way to express his idea in paint, because it was conceived as a painted thing at the start.

In other crafts it is unquestioned that the material being used dictates the form of the conception. If the nature of the material is understood, the work will be more inspired for that understanding. Brackman insists that there is such a thing as an exalted craftsmanship in painting, and an inspired workman can accumulate the knowledge which will not only simplify the execution but will actually be the real basis of a greatly enriched creative ability.

When he says that there is no such thing as figure painting or still life painting—there is simply painting—he is trying to say that the artist expresses himself in paint, whatever the type of subject matter. The same quality of interpretation will go into still life or figure. In fact, more can be learned about his creative ability by an examination of his still life. When painting a figure some elements of composition are already present because his subject is the supreme example of complex related forms, and he need but place it on the canvas with discrimination and set about developing some phase of its beauty. In the still life, instead of merely collaborating with nature, he must create a new theme out of seemingly unrelated objects which he welds together with a magic of his own.

This ability to give each of these still life arrangements a personality of its own is one of the most delightful things that Brackman does. One little thing which he calls *Arrangement #3*, just a basket, napkin and some fruit—subject matter almost as anonymous as the title—is a gay, delicate little affair, a series of linear circles and curves against rounded forms playing back and forth in the most light-hearted manner. It has the character of a happy young child and is as simple.

The *Tribute to Cézanne* is a different matter. Here is a serious mood, quite consistent with the title. Cézanne devoted most of his life to discovering and proving through his work that the artist could render form more powerfully by color than by light and shade. The color of an object changed or was modified with every change of direction. This allowed the artist to construct his entire picture by these planes of color, increasing his power of expression beyond measure. Most pictures since his day have been to some extent tributes to his work.

It is fairly likely that the serene power in the form of the pitcher,

perhaps unconsciously, was a plastic symbol of his towering strength. Slowly one senses the uncanny skill in the placement of this pitcher. By placement is meant not only the area it occupies but the weight of the form as related to the other objects. Only an artist with Brackman's understanding of form as expressed in pigment could have turned the open book into an echo of the color and shape of the pitcher. If there is an overworked and undernourished word, it is selection, but it must be used to explain what goes on here. The curved contours of the open pages charmingly repeat the shape of the jug while the surface of the page echoes its clear surface, but the book is allowed no competing bulk and is treated rather as an undulating plane, a sort of go-between for the pitcher and table top, having some of the qualities of each. The little matter of relating an earthenware jug and a wooden table top by means of an open book is good work, if you are equal to it.

Among our contemporaries, Braque can do it in a totally different way, by destroying the objects as such at the very start and using only such of their attributes as will fit his scheme, but to find this done in the way Brackman achieves it our minds go back to some of the best Chardins before the same quality of vision is found. This does not, of course, imply a similar technical procedure; in this the two men vary greatly because the Brackmans, despite the surface light and shade, are still based on Impressionism. In fact, even the current Brackmans are all designed in areas of color until almost the end of the work, when chiaroscuro creeps in to give more solidity to the expression.

Watching Brackman paint a still life is watching a man doing the thing he most loves to do because it is the most exciting thing he can think of doing. Also, it is a good demonstration in action of some of his ideals of art, and explains his fury at people who try to turn a creative process into mental gymnastics.

The first impression is of the stored-up energy with which he attacks his work, noticed in his alert movements and then in the way he looks at things, which is, of course, the distinguishing characteristic of a painter. Most people look for purposes of recognition or information, but the artist has a completely different kind of glance. At every moment of his life there is a possible picture lurking in the forms and colors around him, and he may at any moment see something that will start him on a picture which will occupy him for months. As a result, he doesn't stay behind his eyes and look out at things. He extends his senses to absorb and gather in anything he can use. Nothing seen is unimportant. When Brackman looks at what he is about to paint or is actually painting, one feels a great amount of creative energy behind the glance, and that all his sensibilities are intensely alert, seeing and relating impressions.

The other part of the picture is the large palette in front of him, where the first impression is of huge mounds of paint ringing the outside, leaving little room to work. Then one sees that most of the mixing is done on the canvas rather than on the palette. The wealth of pigment is an expression of his whole attitude. It is doubtful if he could feel his way through to a picture with starved little squirts of pigment placed neatly about on a clean, varnished surface.

Most of his pictures start from an experience, meaning a visual impression of unusual clarity seen and remembered, not necessarily of certain objects so much as certain attributes the objects may have. A small still life study no larger than this page may furnish the basic motif for a large figure arrangement or, as Brackman says, even of a self portrait. It may even be the starting point for several pictures of widely divergent subjects.

When asked whether he saw a particular apple on the table as a form, color or surface, he answered that one has to see it in every way; not only a sensuous reaction to the surface texture and color, but also to see clear through to the core. It is a living thing, with its own growing form. Then he said, "In every red apple there is somewhere a terrific spot of green."

Most important of everything is the sense of light and life which dominates the picture. The moment the object starts to dominate, the picture collapses. Here is the place the still life tests the creative power of its creator. The subject matter is so commonplace and so heterogeneous that those who run may read whether the artist has really created a picture, or whether there remain merely objects. If it is not the most trying art form, it is the most revealing. The beauty of a still life is the artist's own heart beat, and the strength of the pulse can be felt and measured.

IV

The Figure Paintings

ANY ARTIST WORTH HIS SALT IS SOMEWHAT OF A PARADOX. AS A CRAFTSMAN, Brackman quite vehemently and rightly insists that it isn't what is painted that matters, but how it is done. It is true that whatever the subject matter the result is bound to be a Brackman. This is inevitable where the painter has individuality. Rembrandt painted an old windmill and a nobleman, but what he made of them were two great Rembrandts, *The Mill* and *The Noble Slav,* both of which evoke similar emotions of grandeur which are not necessarily associated with either subject. The great difference between pictures by Cézanne and Monet is not that one may be of apples and the other of apple trees, but that one is a Cézanne and the other a Monet. So true is this that on entering a gallery of the work of really great men the painter of each work can be determined at a glance across the room, regardless of subject matter. Only the lesser men must sign pictures for identification purposes.

Yet when all this is admitted the other side of the paradox appears. Every really strong artist is a man with vital interest in the life around him, and it is to life he must go to receive stimulus for his art. He is a person, and he will be more interested in other people than in anything else in

nature. A purely vegetarian art would soon be quite dull. This reaction to the life around him furnishes Brackman with the starting point for his figure paintings.

For several reasons the great range of this work is not as well known as it deserves to be. The portraits, being commissions, are very seldom publicly exhibited, and the smaller pieces have been obscured by the large figure arrangements.

One of the products of the large exhibition has been what is known as the exhibition picture, which, like the "concert piece" in music, displays all the technical brilliance of the artist. It can hold its own among the hundreds of exhibits and, being an important work, is much sought after by the large shows to the exclusion of the intimate but less aggressive smaller works.

It may come as a surprise to many that several of the very finest things he, or any American artist, has done in recent years are figures of children. Why most pictures of children have to be so very bad is one of the mysteries of art. Thousands of cute little creatures, sentimentalized out of all semblance to anything remotely resembling a real child, turn up each season in the galleries. Diogenes would be sorely tried to locate a single honest brush stroke in the lot. Wherefore it is cause for public rejoicing to find little pictures like the studies of his children, Roberta and Celia, and his things of boys and dogs.

Being a child is a serious business deserving serious pictures, showing understanding of the real charm of childhood. Coming from the studio to the house, a late winter afternoon, we saw Celia inside the lighted window, hard at work playing her harp. He paused and watched for a time, and with a delighted chuckle of appreciation of one worker for another he whispered, "She is so serious! She is trying so hard—it means so much to her!" This acceptance of the child as a real personality is the basis of the authentic beauty of the studies. The one of Roberta has a poise of head that indicates the physical control and alertness she has achieved in her ballet dancing. It would be difficult to find in any contemporary picture as much beauty of characterization as in the few square inches of this study. It is as straightforward as the child's personality, completely free of sentimentality, but charged with devoted respect for the person. When another tiny picture, the one of Celia, was shown in Mystic, it proved, despite its size, one of the outstanding paintings in the show. This kind of result can be achieved only by a very wise and simple person with a deep fundamental sincerity behind his skill as an artist.

One of the most interesting things about Brackman's figure paintings is the way he always seems to find the appropriate means of expressing the particular kind of thing he is doing. Sometimes the solution is rather staggering, when he decides to put five figures onto a 7 x 9 canvas, but as it begins to shape up on the area it becomes obvious that the size came as an answer to his search for the proper way of getting that exact subject stated. As a theme develops in his mind, it takes on a certain scale. It requires so much room in which to develop, and, even more particularly, each figure or group needs a certain amount of space in which to be at ease.

The next picture is apt to be about the same size in inches as the other was in feet; so small that a reproduction of it is larger than the original, yet the thing looks like a large, important picture. It almost seems that, by the time he has decided the size of the canvas and just how the figures are to be placed, his work is half done.

Another example of the one right way of expressing a thing is the way in which Brackman chooses a color range for a particular study, as a musician would decide on how to orchestrate a composition. If the subject is a young woman, the color may take on a kind of glowing quality with soft notes fused into a delicate tonal effect, but with a boy the pattern stiffens up in an abrupt design and the color range lengthens and becomes crisp with positive contrasts of lights and darks. The observer may think this chance, but Brackman exhausted the law of probability long ago, and these adaptations of color and design to subject must be accepted as one of the carefully considered phases of his work. In some of the imaginative allegorical studies the pervading glow of light is as much a basic part of the design as the figure arrangement. This fact receives recognition in titles such as *Autumn Light*.

The present classical phase of Brackman's work is relatively new. In the earlier years he was, like all the young men of his time, patterned on the Impressionists who would have frowned on such monumental generalized statements. They were supposed to be committed to catching momentary and passing effects of changing light and the incidental action of daily life. That the best of them never stuck to their political credo is another matter. Now we find Brackman reacting against this glorification of the casual and trying to find a more permanent structure. This is natural enough, for young artists always found their work on that of their immediate predecessors and then spend the next few years reacting against them and taking the opposite direction, while, at the same time, retaining from their work much that they need. This is strangely like children and parents.

In 1938 Brackman had developed his own style to the point where he could use it for two quite dissimilar results. In *The Market Woman*, a monumental, realistic, story-telling picture, he had not merely drawn the story on the surface, but had built it into the main design element, and had, in fact, created a plastic equivalent for a human act. On the other hand, he was making what might be called allegorical paintings, though they ought rather to be considered as pictures without definite subject in the usual sense of the word. That this was actually what he intended is borne out by such titles as *Two Figures* and *Autumn Light*. When an artist gives such a name to compositions he is saying very plainly that they are arrangements and that we should look for the subject in the design, not in any illustrative story. The *Autumn Light* is, as he indicates, a tonal harmony of warm autumn notes. None of the almost sculptural forms of *The Market Woman* appear here at all; the ones used are forms suggested rather than made real. The effect is more closely akin to music than to sculpture. In a somewhat later figure study he accepts this relationship to music in the title, *Tone Poem*.

There is not much that words can do to explain either pictures or music, nor are they too valuable in describing, let us say, the fragrance of flowers or the song of a bird. These things, which carry a direct appeal to the senses, are baffling to translate from their own language. About all that words can do is to point out that there are many delightful languages quite worth the learning; among all of them, that of painting is without doubt one of the most rewarding. The appeal is directly to the eye, but we are prone to distrust our eyes as messengers and rummage around in our brains for the meanings of things. We get all tied up in knots trying to find some deep significance which, if there, would be a profound visual experience rather than a matter of the brain.

Our own response to these figures tells us that the subject really lies in the arrangement, not in any story. The lyric mood is evoked by the rhythm of the forms which but partially emerge into reality. The artist has simply painted music for the eye to see, rather than for the ear to hear. If left alone, the eye will tell us all we need to know. We shall discover that it is not the thing itself that is here portrayed, but certain qualities or attributes of things which evoke certain moods.

There is a long tradition for this type of picture. Probably the first examples in European painting were made in Venice around 1500, in Giorgione's studio. Before that time, when a picture was painted it was done to illustrate a given subject, generally religious. It was to be placed in a certain spot for a very definite purpose, and everyone concerned knew just what it was all about. True, many painters were straying rather far from a strict portrayal of a subject and were building much of the beauty of their pictures out of the colors and forms of the landscape or architectural backgrounds to the point where there were really two conflicting subjects.

Giorgione was probably the first to arrange a group of figures in a landscape setting in such a way that there was no real subject beyond the mood produced by the beauty of the forms and colors. He arranged two male figures and two nude female figures in the foreground, one drawing water from a well while the others play musical instruments. As subject matter, it was completely irrational. It illustrated no happening, but built a mood of pastoral beauty similar to the Greek pastoral poetry so much admired in that period. Probably nobody ever thought of it as the first easel picture. A new period of painting developed as a result. Pictures could now be beautiful for their own sake, could have as much or as little subject as the artist wished, and they could be moved from place to place.

Another tradition which holds tremendous fascination for the figure painter is the life size, full length, standing single figure. It must carry implications similar to the status of a scholar working for a Doctor's degree because, sooner or later, when the artist has proven his mastery of other arrangements, the desire eventually comes upon him to try his hand at this time-honored problem. Our earlier Americans all did it—Eakins, Sargent, Whistler, Bellows, Henri—all the Frenchmen, Spaniards and of course the English, and on back to Italy, where the other great tradition of painting started. Moroni, whom Brackman has long admired for the beauty of his simple gray tones, was a master of monumental simplicity in just such works.

In 1937, the year after his marriage, with a beautiful young wife as an inspiration, Brackman decided to make his own bid for a place among the masters of figure painting. His *Artist's Wife, Francis*, which hangs on the landing of the stairway in his home in Noank, is the result. It is presumptuous to usurp the prerogatives of time, which alone makes the final decisions about what is and isn't great painting in any generation, but at least it is safe to say that in another fifty years, when time gets around to choosing the fine single figures of our day, it will have to consider this picture as a candidate.

This, of course, is not the only canvas that Francis has helped bring into being. Among others for which she has posed is the figure and still-life arrangement in the Metropolitan Museum, and it is quite literally true that she has been as much responsible for the work that has come from their home as the painter himself.

It has always appealed to him that the things he seeks elsewhere without·avail he ultimately finds in Noank, and it is here that his work, firmly rooted in the great art traditions of the world, has found expression in the simple village life which furnishes all that he needs to bring it to maturity.

Peter Freuchen   Oil   80″ x 50″   Private Collection

V
The Portraits

SOMETIMES ARTISTS, LIKE OTHER PEOPLE, FIND THAT A SPECTACULAR ability is as hard to control as a great shortcoming. A few years ago the New York art world began to realize that it had a really fine portrait painter on its hands, and Brackman discovered that he was confronted with a major problem. The sudden success of his portraits was such that it began to look as if this phase of his work were about to swallow everything else. If he followed custom he would acquiesce, take the course of least resistance, set up an impressive studio and become a fashionable portrait painter. There had been a long hard struggle, and this meant success and security. But the more he thought it over, the more the gold at the end of the rainbow began to look like the thirty pieces of silver.

His decision was to build a studio and home in Noank, on the Mystic River, at the far southeastern end of Connecticut. Here he felt he could control his own future. He would limit his commissions to about three a year, choose sitters who interested him, and determine the conditions under which he would work.

The men handling his work, devoted friends of the artist, thought this decision unwise. The author remembers listening to long conversa-

tions to the effect that he was a great portraitist and would be so remembered despite anything he could do; that it was sheer folly to go off to the country to work in his studio. Success was too hard to come by. The answer, of course, was that Bob's decision, while not common practice, was in the best tradition. The finest artists of every period have painted portraits along with their other pictures, and made of them works of art of equal quality.

The work of the past dozen years has abundantly borne out the wisdom of his course. Also if the future, in its dilatory way, finally makes up its mind to cherish the portraits in particular, it will be for the very reason that he refused to give up the other work, since their one great claim to distinction is that they are what many portraits are not, beautiful paintings which can be enjoyed as such, while the typical commission portrait is like a man's dog—a confounded nuisance to everyone but its owner.

The portrait offers many problems to the artist, but not for the reasons usually considered. While it is actually a very common gift, the ability to get a likeness of a living person is often accepted as positive proof of genius. Children by the hundreds are packed off to art school each year for no better reason. That is not a proper yardstick by which to find the power of the artist. Also it is not a fact that to paint people well one must be a psychologist or have dark and mysterious powers to probe human frailty like one of the major prophets of old. When the painter reads what others think about his mental processes and what he means by his pictures, he is amazed. As Butler said of his critics, "They see in me both more and less than I intended."

When Brackman does a portrait, he always has one or two long interviews with the sitter, at least a week in advance. He stores up countless impressions which, in the intervening days before he starts to paint, gradually sort themselves out to the point where he knows which are the really important characteristics to be recorded. Gradually, human qualities take on visual form. This is a far cry from memorizing features. It is the process of finding a plastic expression for that character that makes any person an individual. Perhaps it is a way of standing, of holding the head, a manner when relaxed, a sudden glance of interest, or the angle of the shoulders. Every human character has a visual manifestation which an observant artist sees and remembers. His ability to grasp essentials and his ingenuity in finding the means to express them is his stature as an artist.

As to the psychological portrait, the artist is an observer and what he sees he states. If the subject be introspective or extrovert, an explosive mass of emotions or calmly poised, it will be expressed.

The painter's own personality also affects the picture because it influences his interpretation of the sitter. Brackman likes people and sees a great nobility in the human character, particularly one that has been formed by an active life. He struggles to get on the canvas the qualities he considers outstanding in the individual.

Brackman leaves no doubt as to whether he is painting a studio arrangement or a portrait. He accepts the challenge of his subject matter: a single figure, a particular person. Instead of cluttering up his picture with endless belongings, like an Egyptian mummy buried with everything needed for the next life, he leaves out all the props and conceives the figure as a complete form with its own type of action. He first acquires that something by which the person could be recognized by a friend a block away; that basic character is the first thing to reach the canvas. For this he needs the help of neither features nor an outline drawing; the likeness lies much deeper than that.

The first few spots that go on the canvas place the dramatic action, the gesture of the total form, long before any features have won from the artist any recognition beyond a single spot of color indicating their placement. When watching quietly from behind while he establishes

Major General Davidson   Oil   40″ x 60″   West Point Museum
Collections, United States Military Academy

the whole basis of character by subtle changes in the power of a color and by juggling a half dozen formless spots in different parts of the canvas so that the personal manner of holding the head and the angle at which one form emerges from another may catch the very framework of personality, it is most amusing to have him suddenly turn and with a grin remark, "You see, the portrait goes on last, when everything else is done." But the real portrait is already there, in the weight and directions of the forms, and the gestures that are expressive of individuality, all rubbed in simply. Nothing is particularized, but somehow the diverse forms have had their relationships so stated that even at this stage it has become one complete form that is a visual equivalent of the character of the sitter.

The full range of color in the form is beautifully placed against the neutral tones of the surrounding space. He never resorts to the practice of having his sitter emerging from the dead black of some "Stygian cave forlorn," a trick which makes the color glow, but, by robbing the form of its darks, removes the feeling of an existence in air which Brackman thinks a portrait needs because of its nature as a picture of a living person.

Character is expressed by the scale of the figure in the space, the placement of forms and the color orchestration. These means are used by the observant artist to translate personality in a way that it can be understood by the eye. It is not necessary to place a bookcase behind a man to show he is a scholar, or smokestacks behind another to prove him an industrialist, nor need a woman hold a teacup far into the unknown future to prove that she has been a gracious hostess. While it is becomingly modest for a child to write, "This is a dog," under his picture, the artist should need no such help.

Another standby of portraiture that Brackman finds unnecessary is the highly emotional brushwork that is popularly supposed to be the sure sign of great creative genius, burning too hot to be held back, which erupts all over the canvas in an exhibition of manual dexterity calculated to take the breath of the observer. An inspiration that cannot be trusted to last overnight certainly cannot be depended on to remain valid through the long years of the future.

If Brackman has done nothing else in American art, his contribution in re-establishing portraits of men to a position of great importance will be enough to assure him a place in art history. American women have, by and large, fared much better than the men. The reasons are, of course, many and obvious. Their personal beauty and the charm of lovely clothes offer the artist every opportunity to make an exciting and handsome canvas. Brackman sees that he can use the anonymous quality of men's

clothes to achieve a severe simplicity in his pictures and enhance the power of his characterizations of personality. Their rich, dark, low-keyed tones support a vigor of form which reveals the strength of character of the sitter, and also expresses as much about our twentieth century as more spectacular costumes have told of other periods.

His men are authentic. They are presented to show not only their physical appearance, but through that their position in the world of affairs. His feeling about character came out recently when a chance remark about one of his sitters brought from him, in a sudden burst of enthusiasm, "My, what a head he has!" The visual impact of the man's personality was still thrilling in memory after several years.

In the life of every portrait there eventually comes a crucial day, some three score years after the painting is made. Then the sitter, the artist, and all with personal memories of them will have left the scene. The portrait will be alone and must protect itself against indignity or destruction. If it happens that it was painted by a man capable of creating a lasting work of art, and the subject was a person capable of inspiring such a work, all will be well. It will stand on its intrinsic merits, be eagerly sought for and given an honored place thenceforth in whatever place or time it may be. As the years lengthen into centuries, it may still live on as the one reliable record of the civilization of its day. For this is exactly what a great portrait in any medium can do. The paintings go back across the history of Europe, and behind that the sculptured portraits take up the record. The slate double portrait of King Mycerinus and his queen lives on here in America, a country undreamed of in 3000 B.C., when it was made in Egypt. This great tradition of portraiture is the visual expression of civilization.

PART TWO

Brackman, the Teacher

I

Brackman and the Student

IN THE BRACKMAN SCHEME OF THINGS AN ARTIST IS A FELLOW WHO spends all his time painting pictures, because it is the most exciting thing he can possibly think of to do. The day when he is unable to paint he is wasting time, and time-wasting, to a creative person, is one of the seven deadly sins. The one exception that Brackman, like other creative artists before him, makes is that time spent teaching others to paint is not time wasted. He does not teach merely to eke out a living, growling the while about what it does to his work. He thoroughly enjoys it and likes the contact with other people interested in the things which he feels to be of the greatest possible importance. He also knows that if the heritage of great craftsmanship is not to be lost it must be passed on by the great painters of each generation to the next.

Since 1938 he has taught a large class at the Art Students' League in New York and conducted his own summer school in Noank, Connecticut. This school is built into his life. First there is his own studio,

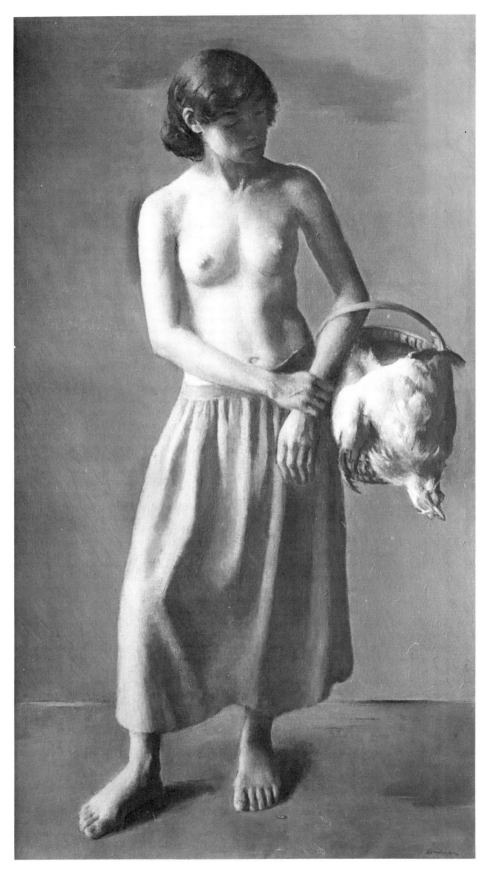

Young Woman and Bird   50″ x 28″   Courtesy of the Collection
of Mr. Haig Tashjian

a few steps from his house, and across the lane there is the large classroom studio, built for fifty students. This arrangement expresses the place in his life occupied by teaching. It is always just across the lane from his painting and his family, across the lane and down a few steps, but right there in full view, a real part of the excitement of living.

His teaching method tells the student a great deal about his craft, and tells us a good deal about Brackman, because his attitude is so characteristic of his whole point of view toward this business of painting. At the very start, the new student learns that no effort will be made to teach him art. Brackman says simply that it can't be done. What can be done, however, is to show him how to become an excellent artisan, and that is exactly what he does. It ought to be self-evident that a beginner must first learn his trade, but so much emphasis has been put on other phases of an artist's work that the simple truth of the matter is that few people really believe that basically an artist is a craftsman, a skilled workman with his hands. While it must be admitted that the proper use of paints and brushes is a factor in making pictures, this is prone to be overshadowed by the more obviously glamorous part of the work.

Painting is often considered to be largely a matter of an outpouring of personality and the expounding of a superior set of aesthetic discoveries. This attitude in a student is not to be wondered at because that is what he hears discussed about the art he sees. Almost no one, talking or writing of any contemporary art, ever raises the question of whether the person under discussion knows how to paint. His point of view is examined, particularly the school of thought he belongs to, whether nonrepresentational, abstract, expressionist, realist or some subdivision of these or other groups; his peculiar type of approach, most particularly his use of subject matter—but seldom, if ever, his use of paint. In other words, a literary and aesthetic appraisal of art is almost the only one commonly encountered by the young student, and quite naturally his response has been to that side of the picture.

Quite naturally, again, in his dreams of an art education he expects to go to a class and learn to live on a plane where all the art philosophies and aesthetic systems are daily discussed just as they are in the newspapers and magazines. He will learn every theory of color, space and form, be able to tell every type of cubism at a glance, know every shade of the differences between the surrealism of Chagall and Chirico, and so on, down to the latest thing bubbling on 57th Street. Then he will find a little "ism" of his own, and, bursting with theories, graduate into the exhibiting field, hoping that the critics will be for a time mystified but that they will soon understand him and hail him as a master.

All this Brackman knows just can't happen quite that way. He puts the student to work. First, he must learn how to become a good craftsman, and slowly and painfully find a technique adequate to express anything he has to say before his work can possibly have any meaning. Whatever value the intellectual approach may have for the layman in helping him understand art, the student must learn from a completely different angle because his job is to learn how to make a picture, not merely to talk about it. An appreciation of architecture course may help the public, but the young architect has to learn to make a building stand up and do the job for which it is intended. The young artist, too, must learn that a painting has to stand on its foundation in the same way, and that, unless the materials are used after their nature, it has little chance to do so. A foundation is not an intellectual credo; it is a good workman's method of construction. A work of art must be created; it cannot be rationalized into existence. Children are not born that way, either.

Brackman's stand is that a student must be taught to see, to feel and to express, but not by feeding him a formula which requires of him no effort but to open his mouth and swallow it. He is suspicious of the countless recipes for painting pictures which flood the art schools. Very wisely, he will have nothing to do with systems of design, color theories and the thousand and one ready-made solutions for the students' problems. He considers them all crutches, the continued use of which will permanently weaken the ability to walk alone. He will have none of them. Nor will he say anything to encourage the common belief that there exists one right answer to all doubts and worries.

To the beginner in any field, dogma makes an excellent substitute for truth and is eagerly accepted. Particularly in art there has persisted the idea that there must be some mathematical formula for beauty—that somewhere, somehow, beauty can be isolated, catalogued, measured and completely proven. Some even think the Greeks actually discovered that mathematically provable recipe. Perhaps science can find an equation to express it and end all this agony of creative effort. Bob is deeply distrustful of the whole approach and will have none of it.

After seeing so many eager youngsters misled, Brackman wants to give them something they can really build on for a mature art. What he offers is no ready-made system with a dubious claim to authority. It is simply the chance to learn how to go about making something with paint, and how to think in color rather than with words. That is a hard transition to make. Everyone is taught to think in words from birth; it is a completely fixed habit. To think in paint to the point where words no longer express what one is trying to say, to the place where an impatience with their utter inadequacy is felt instead of a dependence on them, that is the greatest problem of student and teacher. Once that time comes, the artist begins to learn his own language, and the rest of his life is spent in perfecting his understanding and use of it and in developing his own personal expression. Until then, his language is not that of the artist. This is the thing Brackman tries to give him, or rather show him how to acquire for himself.

Few sights are more pleasant than to see a workman, skilled in the use of his tools, loving the things he is making and knowing them to be good, standing among a group of young people and teaching them how to learn their craft in a way to bring the happiness and self-respect that come only from a job well and beautifully done. That, briefly, is what Brackman feels to be his duty, as well as his joy, as a teacher of painting.

Nude in Morning Light

OIL

28″ x 36″

COURTESY OF THE COLLECTION OF MRS. EVE LORING

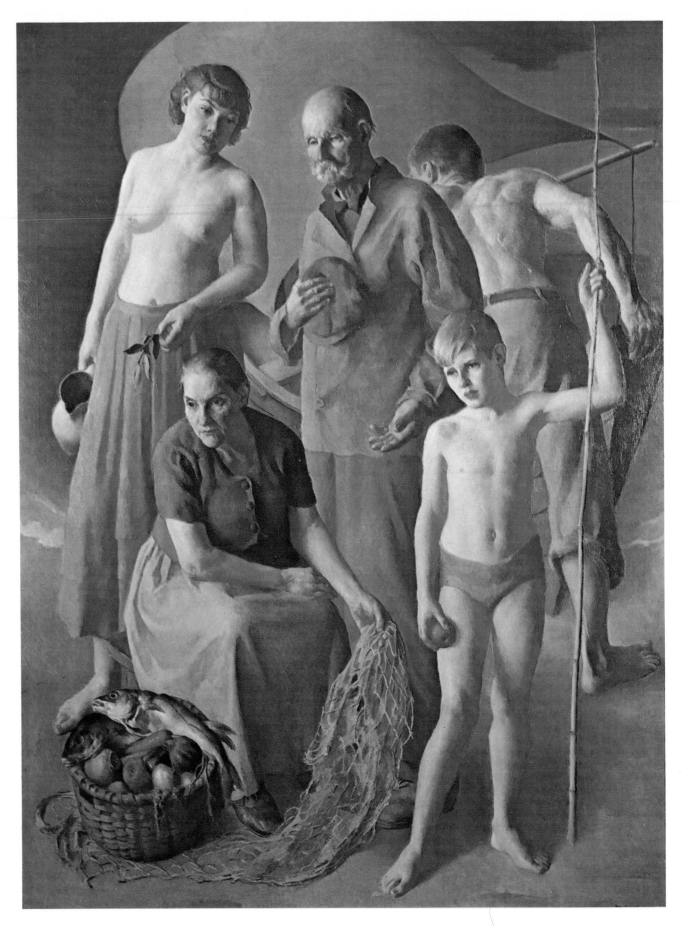

The Shore of Connecticut

OIL
80″ x 60″
COURTESY OF THE ARTIST

The Shore of Connecticut

The Shore of Connecticut

Jennifer Jones as "Jenny"

II

The Approach

THE FIVE LECTURES THAT FOLLOW ARE BY NO MEANS TO BE CONSIDERED prepared speeches in which Mr. Brackman discusses art. They are the sort of talk that comes from an artist in a classroom when he is trying to tell students in words what he means in paint. They are copied from hastily scratched notes, and some of their force may be lost when they are put on the printed page and read in a place far removed from a working studio, removed also from the dynamic voice and personality of one of our great teachers. For that reason the author is interpolating remarks which are intended to call particular attention to certain things which seem of great value in the talks, the importance of which may not be understood by the beginner with little experience. In the classroom these statements are repeated as the need arises until all are aware of their truth, but in a book other means must be used to stress their importance.

The first talk was given as a new class started work. It is simply an introduction to painting. In an art school there is absolutely no uniformity of preparation among the students, who range from tyros to teachers taking a course to brush up on methods, or artists who wish to work from the model again. The teacher must be prepared for anything.

The start of a new class in the large studio in Noank is an exciting occasion. In a summer class in a small New England village there is more of a feeling of fellowship than is ever experienced in town, where everyone disappears at the street door and reappears on the stairs the next day. These students are having an experience and they all know it. Entering the hillside studio from the street level, one is on a balcony and the class of fifty is spread out around the room below. The first reaction is to remember the crowded conditions in New York and wish all classes could have a place like this in which to work. Then memories return of being half trampled to death in one of those League classes and loving it. After all, it is what one is doing that matters.

When Brackman starts to talk to the class there is no doubt that he has their entire attention. That command of the situation that shows in his work is equally evident in the classroom. He turns up in a Basque shirt and slacks, looking as if he had just come up from one of the lobster boats at the wharf below, and the straightforward way he talks only underlines the impression. Some teachers draw immediate attention to themselves; others, like Brackman, focus attenti n entirely on what they have to say. Their firm conviction of the rightness and importance of what they are saying is conveyed at once to the class.

As soon as all are quiet he launches right into a statement that they are in the class to learn one thing, how to paint, and that their ability as artists from now on will be judged entirely on the excellence of the work they produce, and nothing else; also that for them as young workmen the whole intellectual approach to art is out the window. He also warns them to forget the art criticism of the moment and currently featured work which is continually changing, but to go rather to the great work of the past for inspiration because its worth has been proven over a long space of time.

The paragraphs indented here and in the following chapters are remarks made by Brackman in sessions of his class. In this opening session he goes on to say:

> Before we begin our study of painting we have to be aware of the times we live in and be conscious of our contemporary artists, their trends and their origins. Because of the present development of reproduction and the ever increasing number of publications, art reaches more people than ever before. The people who control the opinions of art are the chief factors and personalities in the art world today; I mean the museum director, the art critic and the rest of the professional aesthetes who teach art appreciation. They are also the custodians of the taste of America, and to hold the public interest they feature art that shocks, startles and arouses curiosity, while

Portuguese Girl   Oil   40″ x 30″   Private Collection

they are busily writing books to justify their opinions. They will hail an amateur and place him beside the greatest artists of the past; this merely confuses and keeps the secret of understanding for the few who can agree with them.

Under such conditions you are studying to be a professional artist; however, in spite of these conditions, artists will emerge as they have in the past generations, for they all had obstacles to overcome as difficult as you have. My advice to you is to become a good artisan and let your art, through the right methods of doing things, be judged through the excellence of the work which you will produce. I am not going to teach you art, no one can, but I shall guide you mentally and technically in your studies to become a good artisan.

Brackman's repeated statements about aesthetes are not generally understood. Many wonder why he attaches so much importance to them, but there is a very simple and obvious answer. He is a person who really considers that a fine artist is and always has been a man of the greatest importance; in fact, that he is the only man in the art world of any real importance, since he is the only one who can create the works of art.

He also believes that the student should study the things in art which have permanent value. Only a small fraction of the work exhibited and reviewed in each current year can possibly be of lasting importance. The most experimental and unusual work is featured because it has news value. The more provocative it is, the more discussion it arouses and the more it enlivens the art season. While the student must know what is going on about him, he will learn more from the artists who have made history than from those who make current news, and more from serious works that can give him a real knowledge of art history than from comment on the shows of the week.

He must also learn that criticism cannot take away the value of a great picture, or add value to a poor one. Criticism is an opinion; a picture is a fact. Opinions change from day to day. A great work of art will outlive many waves of varying thought, and go on exerting influence on generations of young artists.

If anyone criticises a study you are making and gives you suggestions as to what you should do, pay no attention whatever to him unless he brings a picture he has painted and places it beside yours. If you are so thrilled by his picture that you want to leave the class and follow him, you should do so; if not, pay no attention whatever to anything he has to say.

Here is the same conviction restated. The only person the student can afford to listen to is someone whose work he completely respects because the young artist is trying to learn how to make something and the only one to tell him how is the one who can really do it. Other members of the class are apt to exert an undue influence. It is very hard to resist the opinion of the crowd. At best, he is prone to be none too sure of himself.

Many students who doubt their talent depend solely on the encouragement of the instructor and constantly wish to find out whether they have sufficient talent to continue with their studies. To them, I wish to say I do not prognosticate any future for even the most promising and talented ones. The fact that you have the urge to paint, that you derive great pleasure from it, and that it fulfills part of your life's happiness is proof that you will continue, regardless of your instructor's criticism. If you have the makings of an artist, you will defy the entire world, not just a mere instructor.

Good drawing and painting will help you in your creative work, and will realize compensation in your life; but if you are not blessed with the skill of acquiring the craftsmanship, and your contribution to art is not vital, then the joy will only be in your production. However, I do hope that with my help you will find some nappiness. People never forgive the inadequacies of contemporaries.

The answer to this question is beyond the teacher's power to give. It lies in the lap of the gods. Some talents mature quickly. At twenty-one Sargent painted one of his best portraits, while Winslow Homer's art matured very slowly. Also, though a pupil be bursting with talent, his very facility may trap him into accepting the easy way and he may fall victim to his own cleverness. By and large, however, painting is one thing in which the race is seldom to the swift. It is very definitely a distance event, not a sprint.

However, that is not the crux of the matter. The thousands of students now crowding into schools and colleges expect to give a certain amount of time and money, and, in return, be assured of something which will guarantee them greater success, an asset which they can cash for money. This, of course, no education, other than certain specific trade school training, can ever rightly be expected to do, and, as an honest teacher, Brackman refuses to promise the impossible. The instruction is there for all, but how it is used is the responsibility of the individual. However, he now tells the student how he can best prepare himself to take advantage of the course he is studying.

To study art intelligently one must equip oneself with a thorough knowledge of its history; not just an opinionated interpretation or a superficial outline, but actual facts and straight biographies of the very early painters, sculptors and architects, their art, environment and the social and economic conditions of the times.

In the study of the work of the past, you, no doubt, will acquire many influences. If your work begins to show influences of great artists, then it is a sign that you understand, and that your taste is improving. The student who fears that his individuality is being impaired by following a great master is usually one who hasn't any individuality, and is not moved or aroused by any great works of art. He cannot acquire any knowledge unless he carefully follows the methods of his master. Ninety-nine percent of the schools are filled with this type of student; those who preserve their individualities and who use the classroom to express themselves, rather than to acquire knowledge. To preserve an individuality and not be influenced by anyone would mean not to see anything nor to study the history of art; in other words, you would be preserving only ignorance and naïveté. While these virtues are admirable in children, they become absurd and stupid in maturity, and have no part in our society. You must remember that the twentieth century painter is a product of eight hundred years of painting.

The art of painting lies within your vision of objects. One comes to school to learn how to paint, but what he paints is of little consequence. You either know how to paint or you don't know how to paint. I often come across students who say that they can paint flowers but not landscapes, or landscapes and not figures, or figures and not portraits. There are no painters who can paint one thing and not another, but rather they prefer to paint one thing to another. For instance, the greatest landscape painter, Corot, was a great figure painter. Figure painters often paint street scenes, including architecture, landscape, figure and animal, all enveiled in an atmosphere of sunshine. However, you shall know more of it as you begin to understand painting from an artist's point of view.

Before I close, I wish to warn you that the publicized, contemporary art that is all about you has been selected and honored by professional aesthetes and art critics, not by great painters, and it is dangerous to consider it as an example of present day art. I would rather have you spend your time in the art museums looking at pictures that have had at least a test of one hundred years, because the heralded paintings of today may disappear tomorrow. The contemporary paintings that are hailed in many art galleries are usually products of amateurs, and although they may give you consolation and an urge to paint because it looks easy, it is for the dilettante and good conversationalist, and not an example for a student who wishes to become a professional artist.

Here is taken up that great bugbear of the young artist, influences. It is a matter of the utmost importance to him. His entire life work will hang on the course he takes. It is true that the novice is greatly worried about allowing himself to come under any strong influence for fear that it will completely kill or at least warp his own personality. Particularly is he afraid of the great artists of the past who are commonly credited with the power of swallowing a student's individuality at one gulp.

Frequently the beginner chooses to follow the teacher's instruction, expecting that he will be told all that he needs to know. He watches the current exhibitions, and, by avoiding completely the art of the past, hopes to have a thoroughly modern point of view. What will happen is that he will enter the art world knowing only the work of the generation just passing into history, but out of style. Brackman tells him what every artist of importance will tell him: study the history of art; go to the great masters of the craft and learn from them; also go to nature.

Henry Moore, the contemporary English sculptor, might be called too experimental, too radical, ahead of his time, but no one has ever yet hinted in public that he lacks individuality or that his work is old-fashioned; yet his great influences, apart from nature in his own region of England, were ancient Mexican sculpture and, of all things, the frescoes of Massacio in Florence, the same frescoes Michelangelo and Raphael studied. The young artist simply fails entirely to understand how he can gain stature and create a more really vital expression of his own day by going for inspiration to a great man of the past.

He has not yet learned that art is a language and that it has a vast storehouse of literature full of the great creative expressions of the ages. He knows the literature of words and the value of its masterpieces. He may even know that studying current best sellers is no preparation for a modern author, but he has yet to learn to read the great works in his own language of paint and learn how they formed it and made it strong and beautiful.

Study for Composition Pastel Private Collection

III

The Conception

THE SECOND TALK WAS GIVEN TO THE STUDENTS SOON AFTER THE START OF the class, when they were deeply involved in the mysteries of laying in new canvases. The good teacher knows that the ideas which really stick in the student's mind are those received when the student is himself making a desperate effort to find a solution to the same problem. Brackman believes that what he should be taught is not a set of rules and formulas to fall back on, but how to think so that he can learn to solve his own troubles and stand on his own feet. He is told that certain habits of work will make the desired results easier to obtain, and that the sooner the habits are learned the better because every day he spends developing a bad habit of work calls for another day trying to unlearn it.

The indented sections are Mr. Brackman's words.

In the first stage of painting, it is important to see that all your materials are laid out before you, and that you are comfortable in viewing the model; then arrange the easel in a position so that the light will angle from the right direction on your canvas, and so that when it is covered with paint there will be no gloss. The palette must be arranged with a full scale of colors at all times. This is very

important because so often students neglect having their colors before them when they are composing with charcoal. It is like having the entire keyboard of the piano before you.

If you haven't a selected palette of your own, you can build your colors around this suggested one: cadmium lemon, cadmium medium, yellow ochre, raw sienna, cadmium red, cadmium red vermilion, emeraude green, French ultramarine, lamp black and zinc white. Upon these basic colors you can enlarge your palette if you so desire.

Be sure that your easel is perpendicular and your canvas well stretched.

There is a psychological advantage in getting everything properly placed when one starts to work. The sense of order created is bound to get into the picture. Any self-respecting workman anywhere always does the equivalent. The point here that may not be understood is the reason for laying out a complete palette of color and keeping it in place at all times.

One might think that as almost no paint is to be used at first one little squirt of some dark ought to be enough. Here is the place where an experienced teacher might well wish to be able to "speak with the tongues of men and of angels" in order to get one little idea so firmly lodged in the beginner's brain that nothing could ever shake it loose. That is that any hope he may ever have of being a success, having happiness in his work, the respect of other artists, in fact anything he may ever hope to have or be is completely tied up with those few mounds of pigment in front of him. If he will but learn their mystery, the gates of heaven are open, but if he tries to substitute some other way to make a picture he is in for torment and failure. It might pay some time to spread the palette and really look at them, and try to realize that from now on they are the words of his speech. They are his destiny.

We shall now proceed with the most important part of painting, this point we call composition. In composing your picture you must be conscious of the size of your canvas, for the subject you are viewing must be arranged within the space of your canvas. Your composition will depend on how well you scale the subject to your canvas and how interestingly you visualize it.

You must understand there is no limit to the number of compositions you can arrange in the same space. If I were to take one hundred students and place them in the exact spot from where I am painting, there wouldn't be two canvases alike in scale or the arrangement.

In composing a canvas you have the right to select any part of the subject and place it on the canvas in any place you wish so as to create an interesting composition. Remember, a good composition, no matter how badly painted, is interesting to look at, and a badly composed painting is a waste of all your efforts; therefore I would spare no time in composing and scaling the forms of the subject until it becomes exciting and inspires you to paint. At this point, I would suggest that you leave your canvas for fifteen or twenty minutes and if you are still inspired when you return, you are then ready to construct your subject.

It is peculiarly hard for the untrained person to understand what the teacher can possibly mean by saying, "A good composition, no matter how badly painted, is interesting to look at, and a badly composed painting is a waste of all your efforts." He senses that somehow it is true, but by the time he really has a hold on the idea well enough to use it he is on the way to becoming an artist. Brackman gives him a hint of the nature of

his problem when he tells him to become conscious of the size of his canvas and think how the subject is to be placed on it, particularly to scale the subject to the canvas. This is something that can be understood by the beginner as a good starting point. Note how, instead of laying down a rule that the figure should take up a certain proportion of the canvas or be arranged a certain way, Brackman leaves all this selection and use of subject matter to the student and gives him instead something vastly more valuable, an idea. He tells him very simply, scale it well. He will get a lot out of those three words now, and the more years he works the more they

Life About Me   Oil   60″ x 86″   Private Collection

will mean to him. That is the simplest, most understandable and wisest lesson on composition one will be apt to find.

It is not necessary to get out a book of rules in order to study composition. Brackman tells the student that he is doing it when he studies the model and the canvas for a long time before starting to paint. Experience will tell him that if he is to paint a week on a study it should be planned more than a few moments. Even a workman making a box does not impetuously set to sawing pieces of wood at random. He makes a plan and the box will be just as good as that plan and not a bit better. Polishing the wood later will help no whit if it is the wrong size.

If it is any comfort to the student, this period before he actually starts painting is the time Brackman himself sweats it out with a new work, particularly a portrait. After about a week of it he has the thing visualized the way it is to be. The hardest part is done.

> Do not depend upon the model to furnish you with the interest and excitement for the canvas, as many students do. They rush into the classroom and are attracted by an interesting pose or a characteristic face and, without thinking, place themselves in the most uncomfortable surroundings and begin to paint in a hypnotic state. Blinded by their mistakes in the first few minutes, they spend weeks rectifying their errors. All the errors of your canvas usually take place in the first few minutes.

> Oh, how often an artist, inspired by a sunrise or a sunset, rushes to the scene and blindly paints, thinking he is inspired by nature to produce a great picture, only to awaken next morning to find a terrible disappointment; thus he becomes very discouraged. This is an incident where the student depends purely on the subject matter and does not resort to his imagination. Wouldn't it have been much better for him to look at the landscape and study it until he fully comprehended its beauty of tones and composition before placing it on the canvas?

> There are no rules in composition. It is nothing but a cultivation of development and good taste. If you take lots of time to study the subject and be conscious of the scale of your canvas before you begin to paint, then you are studying composition.

> The longer you contemplate and visualize the subject before your empty canvas, the more you are enlarging your imagination. Many students are inspired by the semblance of the model, but you must remember that the inspiration that you derive from the subject must be conveyed to others.

You must never postpone the interest of the canvas for another time. Once you lose that interest you might as well stop and begin a new one. There are no canvases of great masters, no matter how unfinished they are, that do not look as if inspired. The reason why I am so emphatic about this is because I often find work in the classroom by students who depend on the hope that it will be more interesting and exciting the next time or in the final stage. If it isn't interesting or exciting within the first few strokes then keep doing it over and over again until the spark is lit and the creation is conceived; with that accomplished, you are ready for the construction of the subject.

"All the errors of your canvas usually take place in the first few minutes." It might well pay to memorize that sentence; it might pay even more to find out why it is true. A writer states his theme in the first sentence of a paragraph, a musician states his, then develops it; a painter does the same. What is put down first is the theme. If it is not ready to serve as such and carry all the picture along with it, it is not ready to be placed on the canvas. Either it is a theme or it is not. Brackman suggests the following test. Leave it several minutes and come back with a fresh eye. If it is a theme, the eye will respond. If there is no reaction, there is no picture. Start again. The student must remember that the audience comes to a picture cold, interested in other things. That theme must be the thing to arrest attention and hold it until the other parts can be seen. The picture can not lean on the model for support. When it is on view the model will be gone; nor can the artist accompany it like a Seeing Eye dog and keep it out of trouble. It must stand alone, prove itself and eventually fight for its own life. If it is to live a long time and have a host of friends and admirers give it strength, personality, power, and enough charm to hold friends until they appreciate its deeper qualities.

Festival in Costume

Portrait of Barry Marcus

OIL
16″ x 20″
COURTESY OF THE COLLECTION OF MR. BARRY MARCUS

IV

The Construction

HEREIN MR. BRACKMAN EXPLAINS TO HIS CLASS THAT ANYTHING THAT starts out as a drawing remains a drawing to the end, and any effort to make it turn into a painting, somewhere along the line, is foredoomed to failure. The result will be without the virtues of either. He therefore shows the class a more painterlike way of drawing, which consists of "putting a lot of lines in motion" to catch the movement, the gesture of the forms, to indicate the way they make the action of the picture, and at the same time avoid the necessity of drawing outlines. He knows that as soon as hard outlines come in, the ability of the student to make changes is lost. He must keep the forms free and capable of adjustments at all costs. All this the advanced painter knows, and fortunate indeed is the beginner who can learn it without months or years of misdirected effort.

Mr. Brackman remarks:

> When constructing the figure it is the best policy to find your drawing with the same medium in which you intend to paint and, since we are painting in oil, we shall begin our structure with the brush. In the beginning, I suggest a dry brush, using any color that you wish.

Concentrate on the motion of the figure and be conscious of what the model is doing so that you can transpose it into the action of the figure, but to acquire the action does not necessarily mean you are putting it in correct drawing. It is merely putting a lot of lines in motion and suggesting the action and drawing of the figure. You may use as many lines as you wish in performing this part of the drawing. Do not erase any and once the action is established, complying with your composition, introduce a stronger color and begin to construct the figure in a more correct form. The stronger your construction is, the stronger your final painting will be.

Here the student is laying the foundation for his study. He might be said to be making notes in paint language, to make sure he remembers the important structure when he starts to paint. One set of lines may characterize the shape of the head, another line indicate the angle at which it is tilted on the neck and shoulders. The most exciting features of all the forms are graphically noted, their movements and weight; everything he wants to be sure to have in his finished picture is here in a sort of short-hand. However, nowhere does he tie himself down to a definite line. It must stay open until the last possible moment so that he can go on perfecting and changing until at last all the parts come together in a unity which is his picture.

At this point I want you to understand the difference between a construction for painting and the correct drawing of a figure. Many students are in the habit of beginning their painting with a very careful drawing of the subject and everything they have to say is said with lines. If you accomplish your expression with lines you then have a complete drawing and it is useless for you to go on painting and, if you do continue, you are but coloring a drawing. If you intend to paint from a painter's point of view, all the effort you put into the drawing is wasted.

Brackman is trying to explain that while a line drawing in the right place is a beautiful and expressive thing one of the worst places to use it is as a foundation for an oil painting. When a form is completely enclosed by a line it is apt to cease to be a form and become an area of a certain shape. In a painting by Renoir one is very conscious of the form though the exact shapes may elude one, whereas if one looks at a map of Long Island one sees its exact shape but learns absolutely nothing about its form. Coloring the land yellow and the water blue is no help; it merely shows where one stops and the other begins. This type of chart drawing in a painting will break any feeling of forms moving freely in space. The

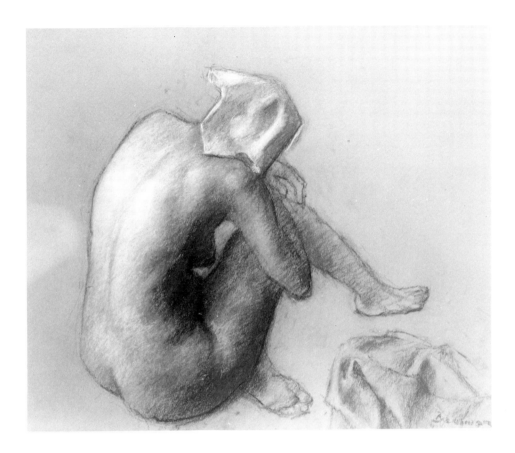

structure lines will give all the help needed without isolating part of the picture.

One of the most frequent mistakes made by students in constructing the figure is that they do all the things that I have mentioned with charcoal and then outline the subject with paint; then they wipe off the charcoal, leaving only an outline or an empty drawing.

Remember that your struggle in acquiring the drawing in the very early stages is the most interesting part of your construction. Once you wipe out this structure, leaving just an outline, you have nothing but a tracing. It is like placing a piece of tissue paper over a beautiful painting and making an outline of it. After you remove the paper you realize how empty the drawing on the tissue is; that is the way your picture appears to me when you follow this procedure.

Even the greatest draftsmen never resort to such methods. They try to preserve every step of their drawing from the beginning to the final stages, never losing the struggle of acquiring their drawing.

Hearing Brackman tell of this noisome practice of making a charcoal drawing, outlining that with paint and then removing the charcoal produced a feeling such as a missionary might have on hearing his converts had gone back to cannibalism. What a revolting result that would be! A charcoal drawing has certain qualities, and a free flowing line in paint might be of some help, but just what could be learned from a timid tracing in paint of a drawing in charcoal it is very hard to see.

Before I conclude the construction of the figure, I want to emphasize that you have to be profound in performing this structure because this part of the painting is one of the most important. First of all, it improves your knowledge of the figure, then, it is very helpful in guiding your painting. The better construction you have, the easier it will be for you to carry on your painting. This is the fundamental and foundation of your final painting. When that is weak, your final painting will be weak; if you master this stage, you will go a long way in any medium you may choose, whether it is painting, drawing or sculpturing. With that accomplished, we shall now proceed in establishing and creating tones and values.

The rich darks rubbed in on the white canvas will compel the student to see the strength and weaknesses of his form arrangement in a way he never could later when the intermediate tones are in place. This is the time a picture gets the quality which, when completed, will make it look good when seen in a window across a street. If it is ever going to have that something that makes people stop in their tracks and stare, now is the time for it to come. Brackman wisely calls the attention of the class to this now when something can still be done about it, because the natural tendency is always to rush ahead to the excitement of laying in the values in a firm belief that not till then will it be possible to see what it is going to look like. A finished building may at great cost have a new foundation put under it, but nobody has ever found a way of putting one under a finished painting.

V

The Underpainting

BRACKMAN'S NEXT TALK TO THE CLASS TAKES THEM FROM THE STAGE
where they have only a structure laid in on the white canvas to the place
where they are ready to start the final stage of painting. This, call it underpainting or what you will, means getting all the values established.
The Brackman solution is that of a painter. By painter is meant a person
who loves his medium and knows its nature and how to use it to get the
utmost of beauty from it. His statement follows:

> In performing this stage of painting you have to be very careful
> in observing the darkest tones that appear to you within the space
> of your canvas. The darkest part of the composition that you see be-
> fore you should be toned in with the actual color, not by painting,
> remember, but by using a dry brush with no medium, if possible.
> Glaze it in with the actual colors that you see. All colors in this stage
> have to be related to the white of the canvas; in other words, pre-
> serve your lights as long as possible. When all the darks are toned,
> resort to your middle tones, then the distant spaces or background,
> leaving the strongest lights that are close to you to pure white
> canvas. Once the darks and middle tones are established in the fig-
> ure you will soon find the direction of your light.

Almost all the things in a painting which the beginner thinks exciting, such as the face in a figure study, are to be found in the lights, yet to attempt to render them while the canvas is still white would be complete folly. Slowly he learns that things are light only in relation to darks and that the reason the teacher makes him start with these darks is that they are the foundation of everything he does, though they attract little attention. Until they are well placed and of the right power he has no way of appraising the value of a single thing he puts on the canvas. When this idea really sinks in, he learns to devote much thought to them. His work starts to attract attention for the very simple reason that people can now see it.

> In creating the tones of the canvas you are establishing the drama and the mood of the picture. If you find that it is uninteresting in that stage, it will probably be uninteresting through the other stages. Many artists have made great reputations just in this stage of painting; not being capable of carrying their pictures further, they mastered this stage to such perfection that they have given great joy to the public. Such pictures are in many collections. I shall call your attention to the paintings of a fairly modern man, Jules Pascin, and you will realize what can be done by just toning in a canvas. This procedure is applied to any subject: still life, landscape, portrait or composition. I want you to understand that this is not a method of painting created by me.

"In creating the tones of the canvas you are establishing the drama and the mood of the picture." The student actually is doing this, with or without his own knowledge and consent, so he might as well consider briefly whether or not his tones are establishing the mood he wishes them to or whether they are contradicting him in public. As with a magician, it is most gratifying to the painter for his audience to be baffled as to how he creates an effect, but if he does not know himself how he does it, it would pay him to make sure. His subject may arouse a mood in him, but if he is to arouse the same mood in the public, he simply must find means of doing it through paint.

> Every painter must understand this stage of painting. It is often called an underpainting. The old masters used to establish their values with just one tone, creating their monotone over the entire picture, but we contemporaries try to establish them in full color of tones as we see them. When doing this, see that the entire construction of all lines disappears except those left in the lights, and please do not use light colors to remove these lines.

Two Figures   Oil   40″ x 36″   Minneapolis Art Institute,
Minneapolis, Minnesota

With that accomplished, we shall now proceed to construct the figure once more. Having the bulk and composition, you will now make a more definite construction of the entire subject and will define your forms more strongly with your construction line. Your construction will probably be more accurate this time and will enable you to define the forms and guide you in placing your darks and lights.

Now we shall begin to paint.

In this stage of the painting Brackman's idea is to keep the way wide open for the student to develop the study in any way he wishes. If left to himself, almost any beginner would by this time have run into enough technical difficulties to make it impossible to go much further. This rub-in with a dry brush gives a perfect chance to establish the darks, middle tones and neutral areas and to adjust the forms to the spaces without getting into any of the usual troubles. At the end of the entire process the painter has not even lost the tooth of his canvas. He has had time to test out and revise his pattern of light and dark, lay out an approximation of his color values and go over his construction, yet at no place has he tied his hands. All his forms are fluid and movable, there are no boundary lines, his color ranges from white canvas to rich darks. He is on top of the world and at ease, his basic problems solved one by one.

As Brackman says at the end of the lecture, "Now we shall begin to paint."

VI

The Color

IN THESE FIRST FOUR LECTURES BRACKMAN HAS BEEN DEALING WITH THE fundamentals of creating a plastic expression in paint. Any student, of any school of art, could learn from them how to strengthen his own type of work. It should be noted that he has laid down no rule that would impose limits on the creative power of an individual. At every step he has insisted on the basic matter of every person seeing for himself, and expanding his own ability to express what he saw. He has not claimed to be able to make an artist out of anyone, but he has shown the class how they may all work to make artists of themselves by building up within their own consciousness a type of observation and expression that will remain permanently theirs and give them a yardstick by which to measure their accomplishment. He calls this developing their taste, but to him taste implies a positive attribute of a creator, not the negative quality of the aesthete.

When asked leading questions about his theories of picture building, the invariable answer is, "That is a formula—I teach no formulas." In this, he is being true to his intensely individualistic attitude, that every artist must stand on his own feet; that great art is, and always has been, the work of individuals. This he believes, practices and teaches. The same approach runs through this fifth talk.

Sailor's Holiday   Oil   40″ x 50″   The Metropolitan Museum of
Art, New York, N.Y.

Before you can understand the painter's attitude toward painting, I want you to examine closely the painters of the nineteenth century. This is very important because, unless you know their work, you will not be able to think properly while you paint.

Remember, I am now taking you through the school of Impressionism, where objects are acquired through values of color. In observing the objects you must cease thinking objectively, or else you are going to draw rather than paint. The construction on the canvas now before you is merely to guide you and make it easier to define your darks and lights.

It would be safer to begin your painting with the darks and think in color; the darkest in relation to all values should be painted first. Do not try to form the object by shading or trying to create a form. Mix your color on your palette, brush or canvas, and once you place your brush stroke on the canvas, leave it there. Do not blend it into a middle tone. Try to place the darks apart without blending them into the middle tones, and place the strokes of color that appear to you.

"Do not try to form the object by shading or trying to create a form." If he were a sculptor with clay in his hands, he could build the actual form, but he is a painter making a picture where there will be the semblance of form created by color intensities, not the actual form itself. Anything he has to say about the movement or gesture or even the appearance of form must be said through his medium, which remains the same mounds of colored pigment on his palette. Brackman is once more repeating that only if the artist employs to the utmost every beauty of his medium will it in turn do him honor.

It will not be easy for you to see color in the early study of painting, but if you search for it and think only in color, you will develop your eye to the point where you see too much of it. You will then begin to look for and compose tonal effects. You will look at a landscape and cease thinking of trees and houses, but rather of the color combinations. You will begin to appreciate the drama, comedy and joy that can be achieved in tones of color,

Color can not be taught, and it is not composed of a lot of reds, yellows, greens and blues. It is a matter of rich values, ranging from the very darkest to the very lightest. Some people have a small range that runs from the middle tones to the lightest; others have a range that runs from the darkest to the middle tones. Some paint full scale, from the very darkest to the very lightest. Even an etcher who creates a drama in black and white could be called a great colorist,

because he can arouse in black and white what a painter does with all his colors. In the same way, the sculptor can create illusions of hair, flesh and cloth in colorless marble. Through this sense of feeling, a painter can produce the appearance of any object by the texture of his paint.

When a painter uses the word *color*, he does not refer to one color or several, but to the relationship of all the tones in a picture. No musician would think of saying that a single note is particularly beautiful by itself. If the student will choose a very simple melody and hum or play the first note, he will see that it is just a sound. Not until several notes are struck in relationship is any mood felt. The same thing happens with the skilled painter. Only when he learns how to relate every tone he puts in a picture, so that together they make a beautiful harmony, has he started to use color. As soon as he does so, a great new source of strength comes into his work because he is then really using the beauty of his medium.

Everything we see we usually see at a distance and in a space, and when we interpret it we immediately create space between us and the object. It not only creates the object but establishes the light that is in it. For instance, in painting a portrait this knowledge is essential, for, without interpreting the atmosphere and space that

enveil the sitter, the portrait will not have the feeling of breathing; without the atmosphere, it will have the appearance of a poster or a sign. Many students make that common mistake and prove that they do not understand painting by emphasizing the figure or model as their point of interest and discarding the interest of the rest of the canvas.

I want you to remember that every square inch of the canvas within the frame has to be painted with as great enthusiasm as the most dominant object of the picture. I judge your painting from the background and the tonal atmosphere of the entire canvas, and not from the subject matter. It isn't what you paint, it is how well it is painted on all parts of your canvas.

Though the observer may confuse a picture with a diorama, the artist who is doing the painting is allowed no such confusion. He absolutely must realize that he is working with paint on a flat surface which the eye sees differently from objects in the round. We humans have a limited range of vision, and it is necessary to focus on a single object or spot on an object to see it clearly. Everything around goes partly out of focus. This is much less true when we look at flat areas such as walls or pictures. What was in nature a very exciting person in front of a very dull bit of wall has become in the picture two areas of colored paint, side by side on the canvas, and are seen simultaneously. If the artist fails to understand this and act accordingly, he is merely being incompetent. When Brackman says, "I want you to remember that every square inch of the canvas within the frame has to be painted with as great enthusiasm as the most dominant object of the picture," he is not talking aesthetics; he is stating a painter's solution to a problem related to human vision.

The beauty of the painting will depend on your tones and color. If your object dominates the beauty of the entire canvas, you are creating a piece of craft and using your skill merely to achieve the appearance of the object, rather than using the object to enable you to create and arouse emotion, or to convey the experience of seeing it in its atmosphere.

If I am successful in conveying to you the painter's point of view of painting, enabling you to see the world through color and tones, then you will be able to define the difference between a colored drawing (which is often mistaken for a painting) and a painter's approach to painting. As you progress with more knowledge of drawing you will, no doubt, discard your construction and ac-

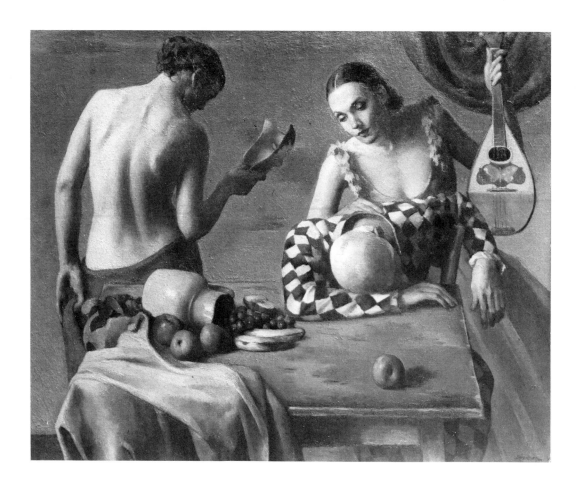

quire everything in color from the beginning. You must remember that the construction is only a guide to keep you within drawing while you are painting.

Coming back to technicalities.

When your entire canvas is placed with dark and middle tones, you will know how strong your lights are and you will gradually fill them in with the colors that you see. When this is accomplished you may resort to any texture that you wish to have on your canvas. If you like your strokes open, you may leave them open; if you like a smooth canvas, then blend them together. No matter what texture you prefer, you will have all the qualities and colors established.

As a student I would not be concerned with the texture at present, until you have mastered all these stages. There is no doubt that you will naturally arrive at a texture most suitable to your temperament and individuality. It will begin to assert itself through tone, color or composition.

When you feel that you have mastered all these stages of painting, my advice to you is to return to your studio and never see the inside of a school again. There is nothing for you to seek now that can be found in any school.

Still Life with Bird

OIL
30″ x 36″
PRIVATE COLLECTION

Still Life with Fish

OIL
30″ x 36″
COURTESY OF THE COLLECTION OF MR. JACK RICHARD

The student by now has an idea of what part of his expression stems from nature. He has had elementary training in taking from her what he wants to serve as a basis for a picture, and in creating a visual theme and expressing it with color, to the end that it will carry a strong appeal to the observer's eye and through it to his consciousness. He has learned first the necessity of depending on his medium to express what he wants to say, and then that his creative ability will be measured by the way he invents means of expressing himself through his paint. In other words, he has learned to think and act as a craftsman.

The student has a right to expect his teacher to show him how to tell a good piece of work from a poor one and how to set about the making of a good one, though he cannot expect the instructor to turn him into a creative artist. He may also expect to be taught the great fascination of his craft, which caused the sublime Hokusai, in his old age, to wish to be remembered simply as "an old man, mad about painting." This insistence on the great tradition of craftsmen in all countries at all times is the very core of the Brackman approach to painting.

Robert Brackman, N.A.

THERE IS A TIMELESSNESS, A COMPLETELY IMPERSONAL DISREGARD OF current trends, in the work of Robert Brackman. His paintings belong to no one life span. They remain undated. Odessa, Russia, was his birthplace in 1898. When he was ten his family migrated to America. His initial studies took place in the San Francisco Ferrer School and later he continued at the National Academy of Design. He had the good fortune of having two of America's greatest painters and teachers, George Bellows and Robert Henri. He lives in the old fishing village of Noank, Connecticut, as snug an anchorage as any man could desire. He is now one of the most sought after teachers in the painting craft.

REPRESENTED IN PERMANENT COLLECTIONS
Brooklyn Museum (Brooklyn, New York), Rhode Island School of Design (Rhode Island), Connecticut Agricultural College (Connecticut), Honolulu Museum (Honolulu), Pasadena Museum (California), The Metropolitan Museum (New York), Newark Museum (New Jersey), Montclair Museum (New Jersey), High Museum (Atlanta, Georgia), New Haven Library (Connecticut), Wilmington Society of Arts (Delaware), Minneapolis Institute of Arts (Minnesota), Canajoharie Museum (New York), Norton Art Gallery (Palm Beach, Florida), Rockford Art Association (Illinois), Encyclopaedia Britannica Collection, International Business Machine Collection, New Britain Museum (Connecticut), Houston Art Museum (Texas), Brooks Memorial Art Gallery (Memphis, Tennessee), Georgia University (Georgia), Municipal Gallery (Davenport, Iowa), Toledo Art Museum (Toledo, Ohio).

IMPORTANT PORTRAITS AND COLLECTIONS

Mr. Charles Lindbergh, Ann Lindbergh; Mrs. John D. Rockefeller, Jr., President Emeritus Charles Seymour of Yale University; Princeton University Collection; Harvard Club of New York Collection; Milton Academy Collection; Mr. Henry L. Stimson (Pentagon Building Collection); Dr. Charles Burlingame (Institute for Living, Hartford, Connecticut); Peter M. Frazer (Connecticut Life Insurance Co.); Clarence P. Dillon; Governor Herbert H. Lehman; Mr. Alvin T. Fuller (Former Governor of Massachusetts); Mr. John Foster Dulles; Commanded to do portraits of John D. Rockefeller, Jr. for Colonial Williamsburg, Inc., Art Students League Collection; President Katherine McBride, Bryn Mawr Collection (Rochester Memorial Art Gallery); General Nathan F. Twining, U.S.A.F.; Peter Freuchen and other portraits for the State Department, the Air Force and for the West Point Collection.

AWARDS

Thomas B. Clarke Prize (1932); Anonymous Prize Chicago Art Institute (1929); Saltus Gold Medal National Academy (1941); Anthenaem Prize (1932); Noel Flagg Prize (1936); First Prize Connecticut Academy (1947); Honorable Mention, Carnegie Institute of Paintings in U.S. (1949); Gold Medal, National Arts Club (1950); Gold Medal of Honor, Allied Artists of America (1952, 1955); First Prize, Laguna Beach Art Festival (1952); Carol H. Beck Gold Medal, Pennsylvania Academy (1958); N. Grumbacher Purchase Prize, Audubon Artists Exhibition (1960); Adolph and Clara Obrig Prize, 135th Annual Exhibition, National Academy of Design (1960); Andrew Carnegie Prize, National Academy of Design (1966); Gold Medal of Honor, National Academy of Design (1966).

ELECTED

Associate to the National Academy (1932); Full Academician (1940). Member: Allied Artists of America; Audubon Society of Artists; Connecticut Academy of Fine Arts; Society of Fine Artists, Mystic, Connecticut; Art Students League, New York; Wilmington Society of Artists; American Watercolor Society; International Society of Arts and Letters; Royal Society of the Arts, London, England (1962); Ford Foundation Grant (1965).

ON FACULTY OF

Art Students League since 1934; American Art School of New York since 1951; Brooklyn Museum from 1936 to 1938. Guest Instructor at

Minneapolis Art Institute in 1936; Instructor, Madison Art Gallery and Studios, Madison, Connecticut, since 1962.

BIOGRAPHIES

"Who's Who in American Art"; "Who's Who in Art"; Archives of American Art; "Dictionary of American Art"; "Webster's Biographical Dictionary"; "Americans," by Alden Jewell; "Modern American Painters," by Paton Boswell; "Art and Artists," by Homer Saint Gaudens; "Color and Method," by Ernest Watson; "Contemporary American Painting," by Grace Pagano; "Pastel Painting Step-by-Step," by Elenor Lathrop Sears; "Painting Portraits in Pastel," by Joseph Singer, and many allied publications.

plates

Roberta Oil 19″ x 15″ Courtesy of the Artist

Boy and Dog   Oil   30″ x 25″   Canajoharie Museum, Canajoharie, N.Y.

Still Life   Oil   25″ x 30″   Brooklyn Museum, Brooklyn, N.Y.

Meditation   Oil   30″ x 36″   Private Collection

Still Life with Mask   Oil   50″ x 40″   Newark Museum, Newark, N.J.

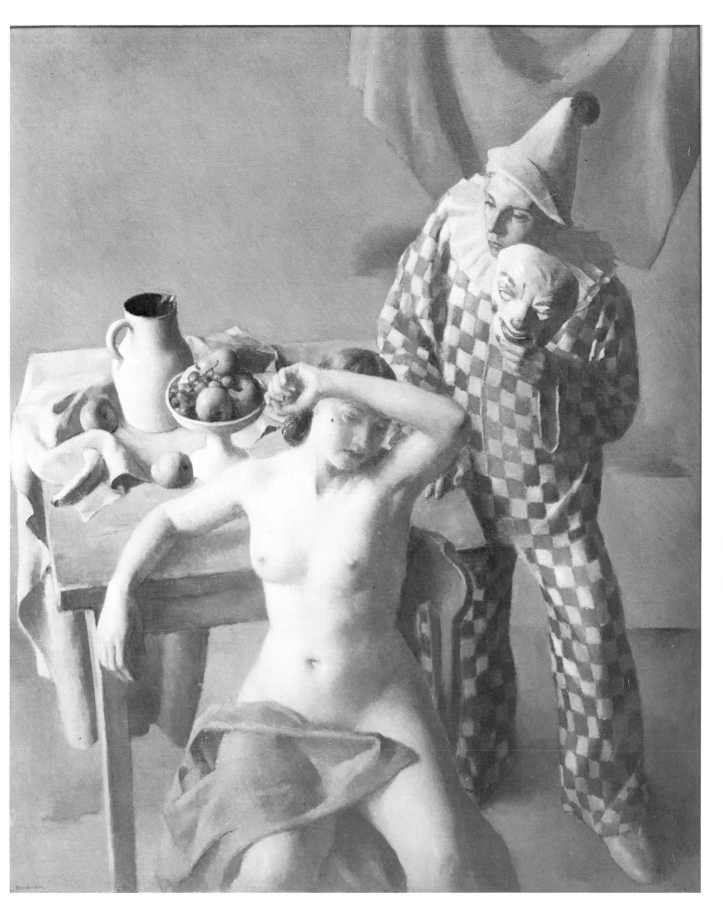

Unmasked Oil 40″ x 50″ Private Collection

Autumn Light   Oil   80″ x 60″   Chrystler Museum of Arts, Norfolk, Virginia

Lady in Blue Hat   19″ x 22″   Courtesy of the Collection of Mr.
Barry Marcus

Portrait of Art Student   Oil   16″ x 12″   Private Collection

Self Portrait

OIL
48″ x 50″
PRIVATE COLLECTION

A Plant for Elizabeth

OIL

28" x 36"

Homeward Bound

OIL
72″ x 60″
COURTESY OF THE ARTIST

Homeward Bound

OIL
72″ x 60″
DETAIL
COURTESY OF THE ARTIST

Market Woman   Oil   36″ x 30″   New Britain Museum,
New Britain, Connecticut

Portrait of Robert Jeffcott   Oil   50″ x 40″   American Cyanamid
Company, Wayne, N.J.

John D. Rockefeller, Jr.   Oil   50″ x 40″   Colonial Williamsburg,
Inc., Williamsburg, Virginia

Mr. Charles A. Lindbergh Oil 36″ x 30″ Courtesy of the
Collection of Mr. Charles A. Lindbergh

Ann Lindbergh   Oil   36″ x 30″   Courtesy of the Collection of
Mr. Charles A. Lindbergh

Portrait of Clarence John Hicks   Oil   30″ x 25″   The Art Museum,
Princeton University, Princeton, N.J.

Portrait of Bartlett Arkell   Oil   40″ x 34″   Canajoharie Museum,
Canajoharie, N.Y.

In a Midday Light   Oil   50″ x 30″   Toledo Museum, Toledo, Ohio

Portrait of Artist's Wife Francis   Oil   72″ x 36″
Courtesy of the Artist

Portrait of Francis M. Weld   Oil   34″ x 40″   Harvard Club of
New York, N.Y.

President Charles Seymour   Oil   50″ x 40″   Yale University,
Cambridge, Massachusetts

Governor Fuller   Oil   40″ x 50″   General Motors Company,
Detroit, Michigan

Study for Portrait of Peter Freuchen   Pastel Drawing   12″ x 14″
Private Collection

Tone Poem   Oil   16″ x 20″   Private Collection

Two Figures   Oil   40″ x 36″   Minneapolis Art Institute,
Minneapolis, Minnesota

Portrait of My Youngest   Oil   19″ x 15″   Courtesy of the Artist